creative

Wedding keepsakes

you can make

Terry L. Rye & Laurel Tudor

BETTERWAY BOOKS

Cincinnati, Ohio

Other fine Betterway Books are available from your local
bookstore, art supply store or direct from the publisher.

05 04 03 02 01   5 4 3 2

Library of Congress Cataloging-in-Publication Data

Rye, Terry L.
  Creative wedding keepsakes you can make / by Terry L. Rye
& Laurel Tudor
      p.cm.
  Includes index.
  ISBN 1–55870–559–7 (pb. : alk. paper)
  1. Handicraft. 2. Wedding decorations. I. Tudor, Laurel.
  II. Title.

TT149 .R69 2000
745.594'1—dc21
00–058561

Editor: Tricia Waddell
Designers: Stephanie Strang and Melissa Wilson
Production coordinator: John Peavler
Production artist: Kathy Gardner
Photographers: Christine Polomsky and Al Parrish

2

I dedicate this book to my spirited daughter Sarah

and to my loving family for their support and

encouragement throughout my life.

—Terry L. Rye

To all those who have made a difference in my life,

especially my loving and supportive family.

To all the people who have gone before me in this life—

for their beliefs, vision and the memories.

And to the spirit of the the white dove—

with love, all things are possible.

—Laurel Tudor

▸ Terry L. Rye

Since 1980, Terry Rye has been the owner of The Mariemont Florist, an upscale flower shop in Cincinnati, Ohio, specializing in weddings and special events. The Mariemont Florist has been featured in the prestigious Cincinnati Flower Show and is listed in the distinguished international directory *Fine Flowers by Phone*. Terry resides in Cincinnati, Ohio, with her six-year-old daughter, Sarah.

▸ Acknowledgements

Many thanks to all the dedicated people in my business. I want to individually thank the wonderful staff at The Mariemont Florist for their support, loyalty and design contributions during the completion of this book: Judy Barnett, Robert C. Cash, Robert O. Hoskins, Donna J. Julien, Lisette D. LaGory, Nancy C. Landry, Joyce E. Sanders, Billie J. Taylor and Jane T. Woodruff. Also, thank you to M. Hopple & Co. and Noriko Fields, Akiko Namura and Emi Yamaguchi for their assistance with this project. I am truly blessed with a talented staff, wonderful friends and an incredibly supportive, loving family.

Many thanks to my editor, Tricia Waddell, for her encouragement and help in writing this book. My life has been enriched by this experience. I will always be grateful to have been given this opportunity by Greg Albert and Anne Bowling at F&W Publications. Most of all I want to thank my dear friend Laurie Tudor for always being there when I needed her. And to my wonderful six-year-old daughter, Sarah, who never let me lose sight of what is important in life . . . our loved ones.

▸ Laurel Tudor

Laurel Tudor is an artist who has professional experience in ceramics, painting, woodworking, stained glass and sewing. She owned and operated a fine art framing gallery for twenty-two years and now lives on a farm outside of Cincinnati, Ohio, with her husband Phil.

▸ Acknowledgements

A very special thank you to Terry Rye, my wonderful friend and cohort since early childhood. We have shared many experiences over the years, and the opportunity to work with her on this book has meant a lot to me. Terry and I have always believed that anything is possible, and that if one human being could do or make something, there was no reason we could not do or make it ourselves.

Thanks also to our wonderful editors, Tricia Waddell and Greg Albert. Their words of encouragement and assistance in every facet of this book has been invaluable.

This book would not have been possible without the loving support of my family, especially my husband, Phil, who has put up with a dining room table overflowing with wedding keepsake clutter. And to my two cats, Merlin and Sapphire, who insisted on helping at every turn, by either sitting on the work in progress or knocking materials off the table and chasing them under the refrigerator when I wasn't looking.

On the top shelf of the china cabinet, a pair of champagne glasses are displayed, their stems trimmed in faded ribbons and yellowed rosebuds. Nearby, a small needlepoint pillow with a few stitches missing lies surrounded by bright green ivy branches that are growing out of an old clay pot. These are cherished keepsakes—memories of a wedding that took place many years ago. The champagne glasses were purchased by a friend of the bride, who took the time to hand-embellish the stems. The needlepoint ring pillow bears the names of the bride and groom and was stitched by the loving hands of the bride's grandmother. The mother of the bride made the bridal bouquet and later removed the ivy sprigs and rooted them in a simple clay pot, giving them to the bride and groom on their first anniversary as a living memento of their special day. All of these items are very special not only because they are wedding keepsakes, but also because of the time and effort that friends and family took to make something personal and unique.

In today's world, it is easy to say we don't have time to make a simple bouquet or a hairpiece—that we are too busy, too rushed for time. We can simply go out to the store and buy everything we need pre-made, ready to go. Weddings are one of life's oldest rituals, and the materials that go into them should reflect the personality and uniqueness of those involved. A long time ago, brides and their family and friends all pitched in together to make arrangements and create wedding items solely by hand. A very important part of this time-honored ritual is the time before the actual ceremony spent with friends and family creating memories to be kept a lifetime. What a wonderful opportunity to visit with Grandmother months before the wedding and sit and chat with her as she crafts the ring pillow that will carry the wedding bands. And what fun it could be to gather all the bridesmaids together and sit around the kitchen table creating the bridal bouquets and flower girl basket. It means so much more when people you know help create a part of the wedding, giving a part of themselves as they take the time and effort to create a warm, loving atmosphere for the wedding ceremony.

This book contains projects for the bride, mothers and future mothers-in-law, family and friends to make, all in the interest of bringing everyone together in the spirit of loving and giving. The projects are intended for all skill levels with full-color photographs and instructions to illustrate every step of the project.

Most of the materials needed to complete the projects in this book can be purchased at retail craft and fabric stores. The floral adhesive used in many of the flower-based projects can be purchased directly from a florist. After selecting a project, read through all the steps carefully. When shopping for materials, take this book with you, making sure to multiply the quantities if necessary. Colors should be selected to coordinate with your wedding colors, and various types of flowers can be substituted as desired. All of the projects are rated based on level of skill, cost and time required. Use this guide to help you plan ahead and successfully create wedding keepsakes you can cherish and pass down for generations to come.

difficulty	cost	time
= easiest	< $50	= less than 1 hour
= most difficult	$50-100	= 1 to 3 hours
	> $50	= over 3 hours

one

In this chapter you'll find great ideas for creating beautiful hand-crafted accessories and keepsake gifts for the wedding party. Create a beautiful floral headband or bridal veil as a stunning complement to an elegant wedding gown. Craft a flower girl basket that will become a cherished keepsake to a young girl. Design ribbon rose corsages and boutonnieres as gifts to all the family and friends who are a valuable part of your special celebration. Let your wedding day be a reflection of your personality and an opportunity to share your creative gifts with the people who mean the most.

accessories for the wedding party

bridal
headband

Perfect for an informal bride, bridesmaid or flower girl, this elegant bridal headband is a lovely hair accessory for the wedding and a wonderful keepsake. Embellished with silk dogwood blossoms, ribbons and pearl beads, this headband is easy to make and can be coordinated with your wedding colors.

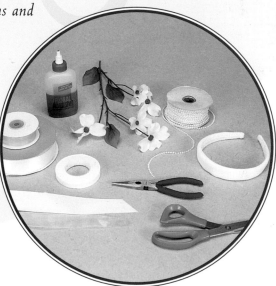

▸ materials

- padded or plastic headband, ³/₄" (19mm) or wider

- 1 silk dogwood stem

- pearl string

- 1¹/₂" (4cm) wide no. 9 ivory satin ribbon (or match with dress)

- ⁷/₈" (22mm) wide sheer ribbon in an accent color

- white floral tape

- floral adhesive

- wire cutters

difficulty	💍 💍
cost	< $50
time	⏰ ⏰

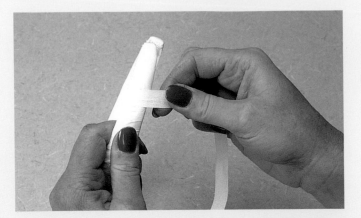

1 *Cover Headband With Floral Tape*

Cut a manageable length of white floral tape and begin tightly wrapping the headband. Smooth the tape down with your fingers as you wrap.

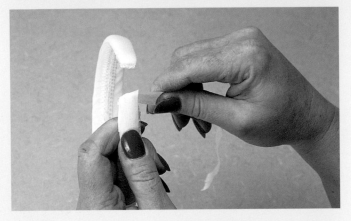

2 *Wrap the Ends of the Headband*

To cover the ends of the headband, place a short piece of floral tape lengthwise so it covers the tips on each end of the headband. Wrap the tape around the ends and back up the band.

3 *Complete Coverage*

Wrap floral tape up and down the band until it is uniformly covered.

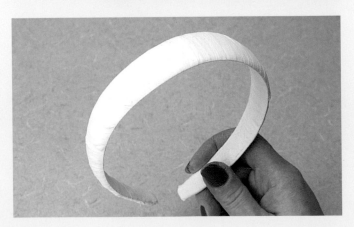

4 *Smooth Tape*

Smooth the ends and edges of the floral tape with your fingers.

5 Begin Wrapping Headband With Ribbon

Place a very small amount of floral adhesive on the end of the satin ribbon and in the middle of the underside of the headband. Let the adhesive set until it's tacky. Press the end of the satin ribbon to the underside of the headband to secure it. Start wrapping the headband in the center, pulling the satin ribbon tightly as you wrap.

6 Cover Headband With Ribbon

Wrap the satin ribbon down one side of the headband, then reverse direction when you reach the end of the headband. Continue wrapping the band until you reach the opposite end. Reverse direction again and continue wrapping back to the center.

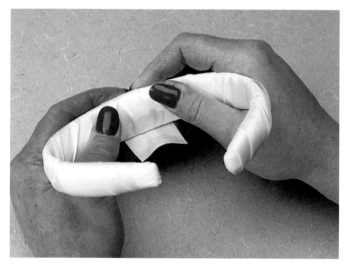

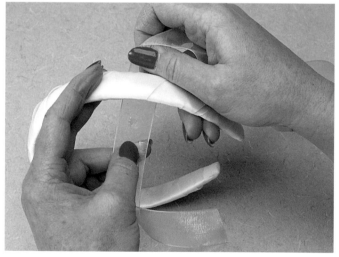

7 Secure End of Ribbon

Place a small amount of floral adhesive on the end of the satin ribbon and the center of the underside of the headband. Let the glue set until it's tacky. Glue the end of the ribbon to the band.

8 Add Accent Ribbon

Cut four 24" (61cm) pieces of sheer accent ribbon. Use a pencil to mark the even placement of all four ribbons along the headband, with the two end ribbons approximately $3^1/_2$" (9cm) from each end of the headband. Beginning with an end ribbon, dab a small amount of floral adhesive on the underside of the headband to secure the ribbon in place.

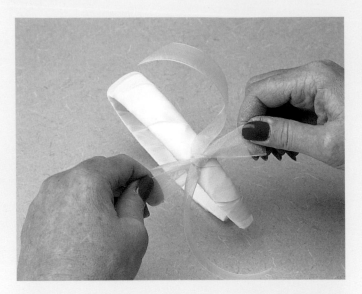

9 Tie Accent Ribbon Bow

Bring the ends of the ribbon around the headband and tie it in a bow. Leave the ribbon ends long for cutting later.

10 Add Pearl Strand

Cut a 8" (20cm) strand of pearl beads. Fold the pearls into a bow shape and lay it on top of the bow.

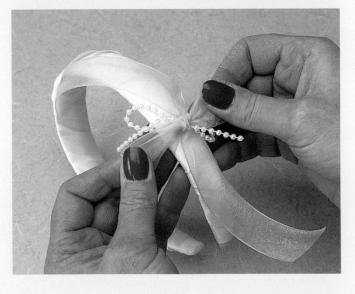

11 Secure Pearl Bow

Tie the ends of the sheer ribbon again to secure the pearls in the middle with a double knot.

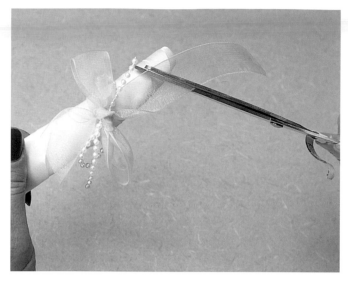

12 *Trim Ribbons and Pearls*

Trim the ends of the accent ribbon and pearls to the desired length. Repeat steps 8–12 to complete all four bows along the headband.

13 *Add Dogwood Blossoms*

Cut seven or eight individual dogwood blossoms from the stems using wire cutters. Place floral adhesive on the back of the dogwood petals where the flowers will come into contact with the headband. Let the glue become tacky before pressing the flowers into place along the headband between the bows.

Completed Bridal Headband

bridal veil

Create a stunning bridal veil cascading with flowers
as the perfect complement to any wedding gown.
Covered in silk ivy and hydrangea blossoms, this
elegant cap veil will look beautiful from all sides as
you walk down the aisle.

▶ materials

- 54" (137cm) wide tulle

- bridal cap

- 1 silk hydrangea stem

- 1 silk waxed grape ivy bush

- 19-gauge floral wire

- floral adhesive

- wire cutters

difficulty

cost   < $50

time

1 Make Veil Cascade

Cut the tulle to the desired length. The veil in this example is 45" (114cm) long. Snip individual hydrangea blossoms from the bunch and trim the backs of the flowers flat. (For flower substitutions, make sure to select a blossom that won't fall apart if the back is trimmed flat.) To prepare the blossoms for gluing, apply a small amount of floral adhesive to the back of each one and wait a few minutes for the glue to become tacky.

2 Arrange Blossoms

Start adding the flowers approximately 12" (30cm) from the top, where the veil will attach to the bridal cap, and leave about 6" (15cm) on the sides and bottom open. Use the adhesive sparingly, and use caution when pressing the flowers to the tulle as the glue will seep through. Be careful to avoid gluing the tulle to your work surface. Arrange the blossoms randomly as desired.

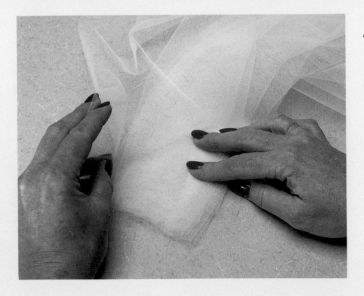

3 Fold Veil

Using an accordian fold, gather the veil across the top and fold it to approximately 4" (10cm) wide.

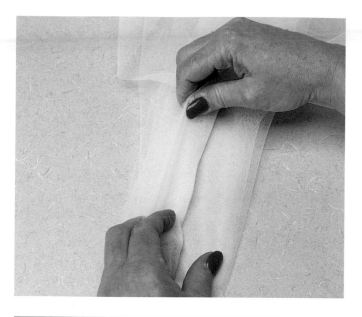

4 Finish Folds

With the top of the veil toward you, take one-half of the folds from the right side and fold them over one and one-half times to the left side. This will keep the tulle nice and flat as it hangs from the cap.

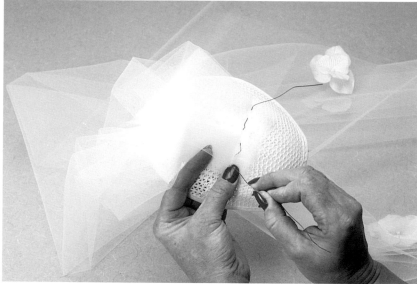

5 Attach Veil to Cap

Place the gathered top of the veil onto the top of the bridal cap. To attach the tulle to the cap, thread floral wire up and down through the veil netting and the holes in the cap with large stitches until the veil is secured.

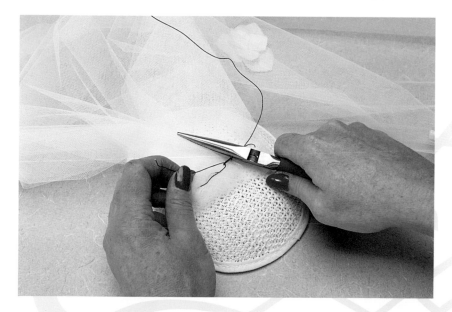

6 Secure Wire

Bring the ends of the wire together and twist them. Cut off the excess wire. Bend the wire ends down flat on cap and mold the wire into the shape of the cap.

7 Add Ivy to Bridal Cap

Snip individual ivy leaves from the stems. Cover the backs of the ivy leaves with floral adhesive and let them set until the glue is tacky. Starting at the back of the cap, cover the entire cap with leaves. Lift the tulle up to reveal the entire cap as you work.

8 Complete Coverage of Cap

Randomly place the leaves to cover the entire cap. Avoid allowing the glue to touch the far outer edge of the cap because this is where the cap will be secured to the head. On the leaves that will cover the edge, put floral adhesive on only part of the back of the leaf and let the unglued points cover the edge. Place a few leaves over the veil at the top of the cap to cover the attachment location.

9 Add Flowers to Cap

Cut individual hydrangea blossoms and trim them so the backs are as flat as possible. Apply floral adhesive to the backs of the flower petals and allow the glue to set until it's tacky. Place the flowers on the cap, allowing a little of the ivy to show through around the blossoms.

Completed Bridal Veil

rehearsal
bouquet

Carry this colorful bow bouquet—full of satin bows collected at your bridal shower—down the aisle at your wedding rehearsal. The perfect rehearsal accessory for any bride-to-be, this bouquet is easy and fun to make.

▸materials

- 15" x 15" (38cm x 38cm) posterboard

- 15" x 15" (38cm x 38cm) fusible web

- 1½ yards (137cm) of 54" (137cm) wide off-white satin

- wide wired ribbon

- thin accent ribbon

- string

- pencil

- straight pin

- iron and ironing board

difficulty	💍 💍
cost	< $50
time	🕐

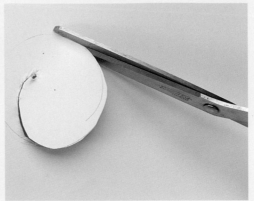

2 *Cut Center Hole*

Using the technique in step 1, draw a 2" (5cm) diameter circle in the center of the larger circle. Cut out both circles.

1 *Draw Circle Outline*

Draw a 15" (38cm) diameter circle onto the posterboard. To draw the circle by hand, make a compass by cutting a piece of string approximately 10" (25cm) long and tying it around a pencil. (Use a slip knot so the string will not wind around the pencil as you draw the circle.) Measure 7½" (19cm)—half of 15" (38cm)— along the string and use the remaining end of the string to tie a half-knot around a straight pin. Insert the pin into the center of the poster-board and draw the circle with the pencil, making sure to keep the string taut and the pencil upright as you draw.

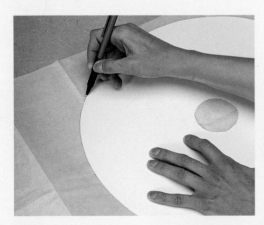

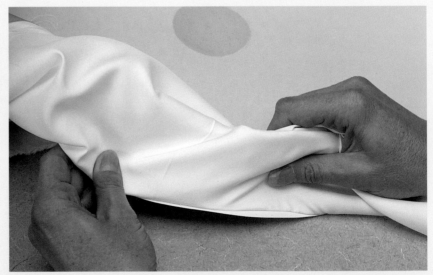

3 *Cut Fusible Web*

Place the large posterboard circle on top of the fusible web and trace the outside outline onto the web. Cut the circle out of the fusible web. Do not cut out the center circle from the fusible web.

4 *Attach Satin to Posterboard*

Cut the satin fabric into a circle. The diameter of the circle should be the same as the width of the fabric (our circle was 54" [137cm] in diameter). Use the technique from step 1 to draw the circle. Lay the fabric face down on the ironing board and place the fusible web circle in the center of the fabric circle. Put the posterboard circle on top of the fusible web. Make sure the fusible web and posterboard circles are lined up before ironing. Using a medium hot iron, iron the satin until the fusible web attaches the satin and posterboard together securely.

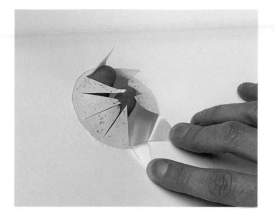

5 Cut Out Center Hole

Using scissors, poke a hole in the center of the fabric covering the 2" (5cm) hole in the center of the posterboard. Cut pie-shaped pieces in the satin within the hole.

6 Iron Fabric

The pie-shaped pieces already have fusible web on them, so fold them over onto the posterboard and iron them down carefully to form the center hole.

7 Pull Fabric Through Center Hole

Wrap the satin fabric around the posterboard and poke it down through the center hole.

8 Form the Bow Holder

Pull the fabric down through the hole to form pleats on the top.

9 Insert Bow

To start the bow bouquet, make a large bow out of the wide wired ribbon using the technique on page 27. Pull the bow streamers down through the center hole of the holder.

10 Secure the Bow

Underneath the bow bouquet, use the accent ribbon to tie a bow to hold the fabric and large bow in place.

11 Add Bows

As you receive bows, add them to the bouquet by pulling the streamers down through the center fabric hole. If a bow does not have any streamers, tie a length of ribbon around it to make a streamer. The accent bow may be untied and re-tied to accommodate additional ribbons as needed. You can also tape or pin the bows on the top of the bouquet and let the streamers drape off the sides.

Bows are often the finishing touch to wedding bouquets, accessories, corsages and decorations. Here's a fool-proof course in making beautiful bows to complete your wedding keepsakes.

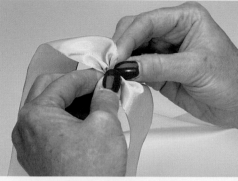

1 Begin by pinching the ribbon (still on the bolt) between your fingers approximately 12" (30cm) from the end of the ribbon. That endpiece of ribbon will become the first streamer of the bow. If 12" (30cm) is not long enough for what you are making pinch further up the ribbon and make it as long as you desire.

2 To make the center loop of the bow, twist the ribbon with your fingers and form a small hoop. Pinch the ribbon together in the center with your beginning streamer.

3 Continue to hold the bow in the center and twist the leading part of your ribbon. Make a larger loop that will become the start of your actual bow. The size of the loop will determine the width of your bow. As you complete the loop, bring the ribbon back to the center of the bow.

4 Twist the ribbon in the center before beginning each new loop. Keep making loops from side to side until your bow is as full as desired. Four to five loops on a side are a common size. Keep holding the bow in the center with pinched fingers and cut your ribbon from the bolt to approximately the same length as your starting streamer.

5 Secure your bow by threading a floral wire through it. Pull the wire evenly through the bow, bring the wire ends to the back of the bow and twist tightly around the center of the bow.

6 Now you have a finished bow. If you want to add more streamers, cut a piece of ribbon about twice the length (but not exactly) of the existing streamers. Streamers look better when they are of varying lengths. Pinch the center of the additional ribbon streamer and secure it with the wire holding the bow together. Adjust the loops attractively on both sides and trim the ends of the streamers with a diagonal or V-cut.

ribbon rose
corsage & boutonniere

Honor the family and friends taking part in your wedding by creating stylish ribbon rose corsages and boutonnieres. Not only can they be coordinated with your wedding colors, but they make wonderful keepsake gifts as well.

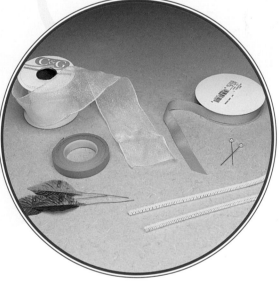

⟶ materials

- 1 yard (90 cm) of 2$\frac{1}{4}$"(6cm) wide sheer wired ribbon for each ribbon rose

- $\frac{1}{2}$ yard (45cm) of 2$\frac{1}{4}$" (6cm) wide sheer wired ribbon for each ribbon rosebud

- $\frac{3}{4}$ yard (69cm) of 2$\frac{1}{4}$" (6cm) wide sheer wired ribbon for each boutonniere

- $\frac{5}{8}$" (16cm) moss green grosgrain ribbon

- silk corsage leaves

- 2" (5cm) corsage pins

- moss green floral tape

- white chenille stems (or 24-gauge floral wire)

- pencil

difficulty	💍 💍 💍
cost	< $50
time	⏰

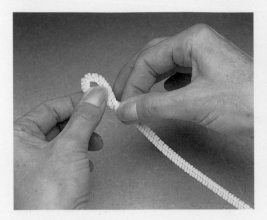

1 *Make a Loop*

Make a small loop on the end of a chenille stem. Twist the end around the stem of the chenille stem to secure the loop.

2 *Gather Wired Ribbon*

Hold one end of the wire on one side of the wired ribbon and work the ribbon back along the wire until approximately 1" (2.5cm) of wire is exposed.

3 *Fold Ribbon*

Fold the ribbon over the chenille stem loop as shown.

4 *Secure Ribbon*

Gather the ribbon close to the chenille stem at the base of the loop and wrap the exposed wire around the ribbon to attach it to the chenille stem.

5 *Form the Petals*

Bring the ribbon up the chenille stem loop and wrap it around the center ribbon fold, leaving it loose at the top. Begin to twist the ribbon to form petals.

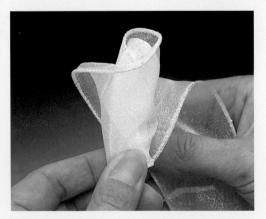

6 *Form Center Bud*

Wrap the ribbon around the center of the flower, twisting down to form the petals. Hold each twist in place with your other hand. Make two complete rotations around the flower center to form the middle of the rose.

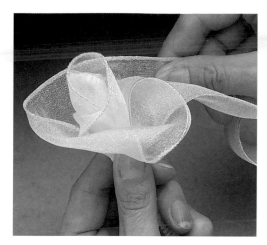

7 Complete Rose Petals

Continue twisting and wrapping the ribbon to form petals while holding the bottom edges of the petals in place with your fingers. If the ribbon starts to slide down the chenille stem, just pull the chenille stem loop back down into the center of the rose and arrange the ribbon petals as desired. Continue forming the petals until you reach the end of the ribbon.

8 Secure Rose With Floral Tape

Wrap floral tape around the base of the rose so it holds all the ribbon petals firmly. The tape is activated by the heat in your hands, so be sure to smooth it down with your fingers as you wrap. Continue to wrap the tape down the length of the chenille stem.

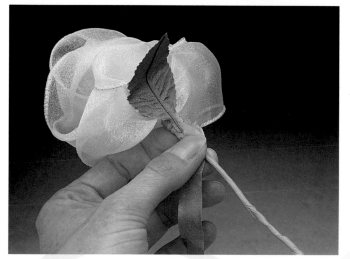

9 Attach Corsage Leaves

Position a corsage leaf as desired and use floral tape to hold it in place, making sure to cover the entire length of the leaf stem wire. Tear off the floral tape and smooth it down with your fingers.

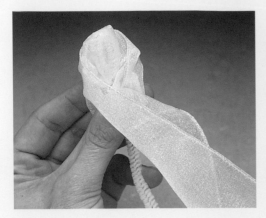

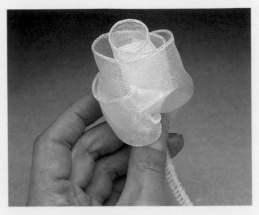

10 *Form Rosebud*

To make a rosebud, use a ½ yard (46cm) of ribbon and the technique in steps 1–7, but keep the ribbon petals closer to the chenille stem to make the flower small.

11 *Add Corsage Leaf*

Tape the stem and petals in place and add a corsage leaf using the technique in step 9.

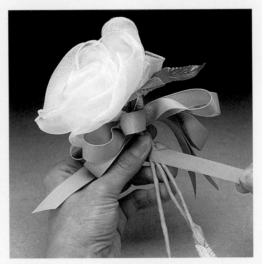

12 *Make Bow*

Make a ribbon bow to your desired size requirements using the technique on page 27. Use a chenille stem or floral wire to secure and form the stem of the bow. Wrap the bow stem with floral tape using the techniques described in steps 8 and 9.

13 *Tape Flowers and Bow*

Hold both the ribbon rose and ribbon rosebud together and position the bow at the base of the roses as desired. Wrap all three together at the base with floral tape to secure the arrangement.

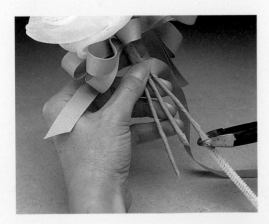

14 *Cut Stems*

Cut the stems off at approximately 4" (10cm).

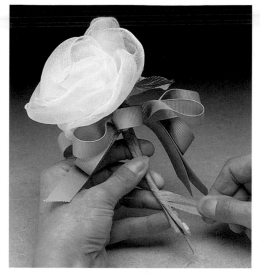

15 Finish Wrapping Stems

Finish wrapping all three stems tightly with floral tape, then tear off the floral tape at the end. Smooth the stem with your fingers.

16 Curl Stem

Curl the stem around a pencil into a spiral. Insert two corsage pins through the stem.

17 Create Boutonniere

The above steps detail how to make a corsage. To make a boutonniere, follow steps 1–9 for the ribbon rose, but keep the rose smaller by using a shorter length of ribbon. Wrap a corsage leaf into the stem and finish off the stems the same as the corsage. Next, coil the stem around a pencil. Omit the bow on the boutonniere and insert one corsage pin through the stem.

silk floral
pomander

A charming alternative for a flower girl, this floral pomander is perfect for a garden wedding. Designed with silk alstroemeria, silk yarrow, silk ivy and moss, the pomander is as beautiful as it is durable. And it will make a delightful keepsake gift for your little flower girl.

▸ **materials**

• 2 stems silk alstroemeria

• 2–4 stems silk yarrow

• 2–3 stems silk ivy

• sphagnum moss

• 5" (13cm) foam ball

• ¹/₄" (6cm) wide picot ribbon

• floral adhesive

• 24-gauge floral wire

difficulty

cost   < *$50*

time

1 Cut Picot Ribbon

Cut a length of picot ribbon 48" (122cm) long. Loop the ribbon in half and bring the ends together so they are even. Poke a strand of floral wire through both ribbons approximately $\frac{1}{2}$" (13mm) from the ends.

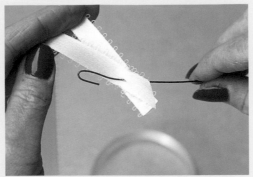

2 Make Wire Loop

Make a loop in one end of the wire about $\frac{1}{2}$" (13mm) long. Squeeze the wire loop tightly around the ribbon ends, making sure to keep the wire loop straight.

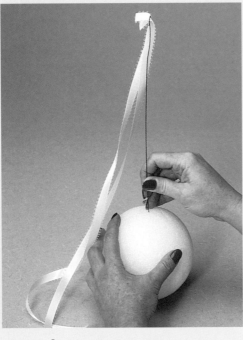

3 Push Wire Through Ball

Push the wire through the foam ball, making sure the wire travels straight from top to bottom. Place the foam ball on a hard surface and push the wire down until it stops—this helps ensure the wire travels in a straight path. If the wire is not straight through the ball, try again.

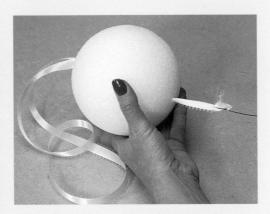

4 Pull Ribbon Through Ball

Pull the wire through the ball until the ribbon emerges. Pull about 4" (10cm) of ribbon out. Do not cut the ribbon at this time.

5 Cover Ball With Moss

Soak the sphagnum moss in water. Squeeze out the excess water before using it. Apply floral adhesive to the foam ball and let the glue set for a few minutes until it gets tacky. Cover the ball with moss, pressing the moss firmly onto the ball. Any moss that hangs loose may be glued down or trimmed off as desired.

6 Add Ivy

Cut small sprigs of ivy and poke the stems into the foam ball to cover as desired.

7 Hang Pomander

While completing the ivy, it may be helpful to hang the ball so you can turn and view it from all sides.

8 Add Alstroemeria

Cut small stems of alstroemeria and insert them around the top of the foam ball.

9 Add Yarrow

Cut small sprigs of yarrow and push the stems into the ball at various depths. Place yarrow in lines cascading down and around from the top to make it look as if flowers are trailing around the ball. (Note: Silk or dried baby's breath may be substituted for yarrow.)

10 Adjust Loop

Hold the pomander and pull the ribbon through the foam ball until approximately 5" to 7" (13cm to 18cm) of the loop is left at the top. This loop may be adjusted if necessary for the height of the child. Any portions of ribbon that have gotten glue on them will be pulled through and hidden in this step. Tie a square knot at the base of the foam ball, tie slip knots in each ribbon and trim the ends as desired.

flower girl
basket

Present your flower girl with this delightful basket

covered in silk delphinium and silk ivy. Add delicate

satin ribbon bows and fill it with fresh rose petals,

potpourri or confetti to be sprinkled down the aisle.

materials

- 2 stems silk delphinium

- 1 silk ivy bush with waxed leaves

- $\frac{1}{8}$" (3mm) wide satin ribbon

- $\frac{5}{8}$" (16mm) wide picot ribbon

- 18" (46cm) of 12" (30cm) wide tulle

- basket with handle

- floral adhesive

- 19-gauge floral wire

- wire cutters

- fresh or silk rose petals, potpourri or confetti

difficulty

cost   *< $50*

time

1 Apply Adhesive to Ivy

Cut individual ivy leaves from the stems, trimming each leaf stem off completely flush with the leaf body. Apply floral adhesive to cover the entire back of each ivy leaf and let stand for a few minutes until the glue is tacky.

2 Cover Basket With Ivy Leaves

Press the preglued ivy leaves onto the basket, overlapping the leaves until the outside of the basket is completely covered. (Note: Alternating the direction of the ivy leaves makes for a more natural look.)

3 Leave Opening Around Handle

Leave a small open space at the base of the handle on each side of the basket so that the bows can be secured to the handle later. Wrap the leaf edges onto the bottom of the basket.

4 Attach Ivy to Basket Edges

Attach ivy leaves on either side of the basket handles. Wrap the leaf edges over the rim of the basket and use small ivy leaves to cover any small spaces between leaves.

5 Add Ivy to Handle

Find four large ivy leaves that are the same shape and size and glue them on either side of the handle base. Do this on both ends of the handle. Be sure to leave a small space for floral wire to be inserted to attach the bows.

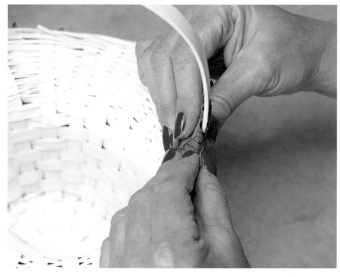

6 Glue Leaves Together

Press the overlapping preglued edges of the two leaves together on each side.

7 Add Adhesive to Delphinium Blossoms

Trim individual delphinium blossoms from the stems using the wire cutters. Trim the backs of the flowers as close as possible so the blossoms lie flat against the basket. Apply floral adhesive to the backs of the petals and let the glue set a few minutes until it's tacky. Place delphinium blossoms randomly all over the basket.

9 *Add Bows*

Following the technique on page 27, make two bows combining both types of ribbon and secure the loops with floral wire. Thread one end of the wire behind each handle just below the side leaves.

8 *Cover Basket With Blossoms*

Apply the flower blossoms around the entire basket base, and remember to leave an open space at the handle base to attach the ribbon.

10 *Secure Bows With Wire*

Pull the wire through the basket until the bow is centered over each handle. Twist the two wire ends together to secure the bows on both sides.

11 *Complete Bow*

Trim the ends of the bow wire tie with wire cutters, and bend the ends back against the basket out of sight.

12 *Add Tulle*

Bunch up some tulle and insert it into the bottom of the basket as a support for the flower petals. Fill the basket with fresh or silk rose petals, potpourri or confetti.

ribbon rose
halo

Create this beautiful ribbon rose halo for a flower girl, bridesmaid or bride. Use silk ivy, silk baby's breath, glass beads and ribbon to finish off this romantic hair accessory.

materials

- 2 stems silk ivy
- 1 stem silk baby's breath
- ³/₄" (19mm) wide sheer ribbon
- ¹/₄" (6mm) wide gold ribbon
- 24-gauge bead wire
- white and silver glass seed beads
- pearl beads
- 8" x 10" (20cm x 25cm) single-sided corrugated cardboard

- paddle wire (comes on a paddle for ease of handling)
- white floral tape
- green floral tape
- 24-gauge floral wire
- floral adhesive
- wire cutters
- pencil

difficulty

cost < $50

time

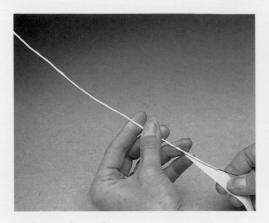

1 Wrap Wire With Floral Tape

Using white floral tape, wrap the entire length of a floral wire. Hold the tape in one hand and twist the wire and smooth the tape with the fingers of the other hand.

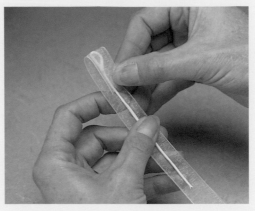

2 Make a Loop

After wrapping the wire, cut it to approximately 5" (13cm). (Save the rest of the taped wire.) Make a loop at one end and twist the wire end around to secure the loop. Cut 24" (61cm) of sheer ribbon and fold one end of the ribbon over the wire loop.

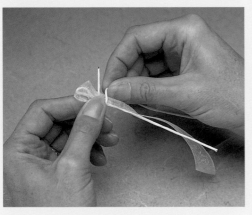

3 Secure Ribbon

Twist the rest of the wrapped wire around the ribbon at the base of the loop to hold it in place.

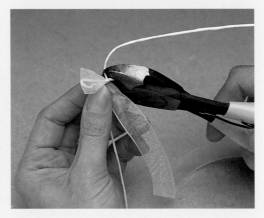

4 Cut Excess Wire

Cut off the excess wire close to the ribbon with wire cutters.

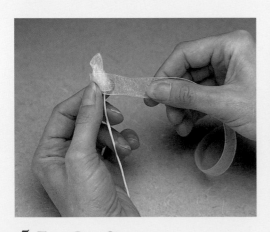

5 Form Rose Center

Begin wrapping the ribbon around the loop to form the center of the ribbon rose.

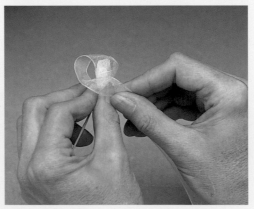

6 Form Petals

Twist the ribbon one full turn to form each petal and gather the lower part securely around the loop with your fingers.

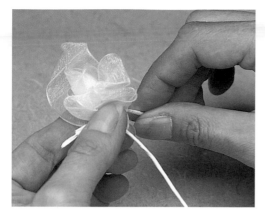

7 Wire Completed Rose

Once the ribbon rose is formed, secure the petals at the base of the loop by using the remainder of the taped floral wire. Twist the wire securely around the ribbon and cut off any excess wire.

8 Wrap Stem

Using green floral tape, wrap the base of each ribbon rose and continue to wrap tape down the stem. Use the heat from your fingers to adhere and smooth the tape as you wrap. Tear off the tape when you reach the end and smooth it down. Repeat steps 1–8 to complete a total of six ribbon roses.

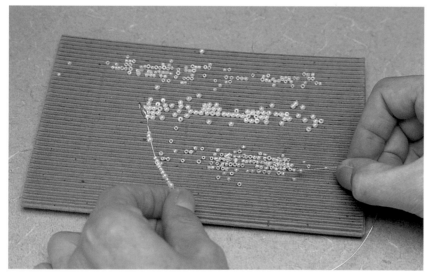

9 Create Beaded Accents

Once you have completed the ribbon roses, you can begin making the bead accents. Pour your beads onto a piece of corrugated cardboard to make it easy to thread them. Use a 15" (38cm) length of bead wire to thread the beads, alternating the seed and pearl beads. After the first bead is strung, wrap approximately ¼" (6mm) of the end of the wire back around the bead to keep the beads from sliding off the end. When you have strung the wire with beads up to 10" (25cm), wrap the wire around the last bead to hold it securely and cut the wire.

10 Create Spiral

Wrap the completed bead wire around a pencil to form a spiral.

11 Wire Bead Accents

Cut two 8" (20cm) pieces of bead wire and loop one through each end of the bead wire and fold the wire back on itself to link securely. Wrap each end in green floral tape. Repeat steps 9–11 to complete a total of three bead accents.

12 Measure Halo Frame

Measure head for halo then cut two pieces of paddle wire as follows: Wire A should be the measured length for the head plus 2" (5cm). Wire B should be 6" (15cm) longer than Wire A. Wrap each wire with green floral tape and smooth with your fingers.

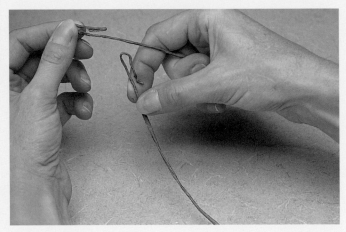

13 Make Loops

Make a 1" (2.5cm) loop in both ends of wire A.

14 *Add Ivy*

Cut two stems of ivy apart to form sprigs with two to three leaves each. Place a sprig of ivy on wire A and wrap wire B around the ivy stems to secure it to wire A. Continue adding sprigs of ivy to wire A and wrap them securely with wire B along the entire length.

15 *Complete Ivy*

After wrapping all of the ivy, cut off any excess wire from wire B.

16 *Add Baby's Breath*

Cut two stems of baby's breath into small sprigs. Using floral adhesive, place baby's breath stems into the holes between wires A and B. Intersperse the baby's breath between the ivy as desired.

17 *Add Ribbon Roses*

Secure the ribbon roses to the halo by wrapping the wire stems around the halo. Hide the ends of the stems in the ivy or cut off the excess wire.

18 Add Beaded Spirals

Secure the beaded spirals to the halo by wrapping the taped bead wire ends around the halo securely. Hide the ends of the wires in the ivy or cut off the excess wire.

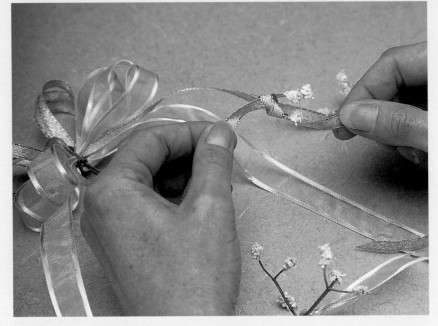

19 Add Bow

Follow the instructions on page 27 to make a bow combining the sheer and gold ribbon. Use a strand of floral wire wrapped with green floral tape to secure the bow in the center, and leave approximately 4" (10cm) of wire to form a stem for the bow. Tie sprigs of baby's breath randomly on the streamers with slip knots.

20 _Secure Bow to Halo_

Slide the bow through the loop at one end of the halo (wire A) and secure it by wrapping the wire stem back into the halo and hiding it in the ivy. Cut off any excess wire if necessary. Hook the two end loops of the halo together to complete the halo. To adjust the size, alter the size of the loops on the ends.

Completed Ribbon Rose Halo

two

All your wedding dreams are about to come true. You want everything to be beautiful, romantic and enchanting, and the moment has come to define the mood and style for your wedding. This chapter will assist you in creating decorations and keepsakes that will add personality, romance and charm to the wedding celebration. A wedding is a good time to explore your creativity, imagination and individualism. The projects in this section will help you transform your fantasies into reality. Message Baskets make wonderful reception table centerpieces, allowing your guests to write down their wedding wishes for a long and full life together. The Bride and Groom Chairs can add elegance to the head table, and the Satin Champagne Pouch and Floral Napkin Rings will dress up the table beautifully. This is your special day, so select the keepsake projects that mean the most to you and plan ahead. Each item you create yourself will become a cherished memento because it was made with care and love in your own personal style.

wedding
dreams to
reality

satin
champagne pouch

Dress up the head table at the reception with this satin champagne pouch. Weave inexpensive wired ribbon together and finish it off with elegant cording to create a stylish table accessory for your wedding celebration that also makes a lovely gift bag.

◆ materials

- 1¼" (3cm) wide satin wired ribbon

- fusible web or 1" (2.5cm) wide fusible web seam tape

- 24" (61cm) cording with tassel tie

- iron and ironing board

difficulty	💍 💍 💍 💍 💍
cost	< $50
time	🕐 🕐 🕐

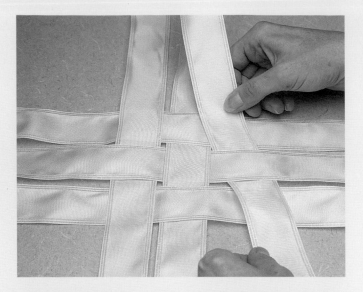

1 Form the Base of the Pouch

Cut six strips of ribbon to the length equaling double the height of the bottle plus 12" (30cm). Interweave the ribbon using a simple over and under weaving technique with three strips vertical and three strips horizontal.

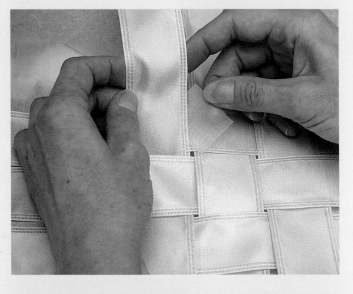

2 Insert Fusible Web

Cut 1" (2.5cm) squares of fusible web and insert where the ribbons overlap. To insert a square of fusible web, position it under vertical ribbons where they overlap horizontal ribbons. It is not necessary to place a piece of fusible web under every overlapping piece, but it is fine to do so if you prefer. By placing the fusible web under every other square of ribbon, the pouch will have a fluffier appearance than if the web is placed underneath every square.

3 Iron Fusible Web

When each fusible web square has been positioned evenly under the overlapping sections of ribbon, press the ribbon with a warm iron to activate it and adhere the ribbon strips together. In this case, the fusible web is placed in a checkerboard fashion underneath the overlapping sections of the vertical strips.

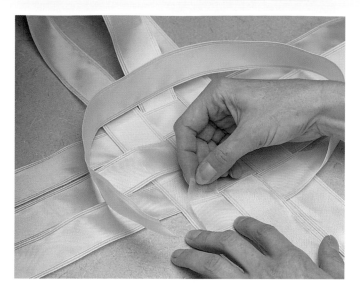

4 Begin First Row of Pouch Body

Cut eight strips of ribbon 24" (61cm) long. These will be used to weave the body of the pouch. Start the first row by weaving one end of the ribbon through one side of the three vertical strips as shown. Place a square of fusible web under each of the two end squares of the vertical ribbon.

5 Secure Ribbon

Iron both squares of fusible web to secure the first row of ribbon.

6 Continue Weaving

Continue to weave the ribbon around the base on the next side, this time placing a square of fusible web underneath the center strip of ribbon. As you continue weaving the body of the pouch, you will be placing the fusible web underneath every other square of the ribbons creating the rows. One side will be fused under the two outside squares, the second side will be fused under the center square, the third side will be fused under the two outside squares, and the fourth side will be fused underneath the center square. Note that, starting with the second side, you will need to shape the ribbons into a pouch.

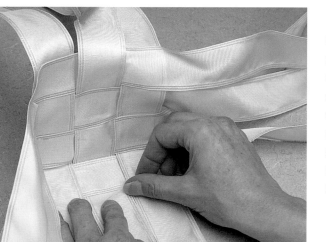

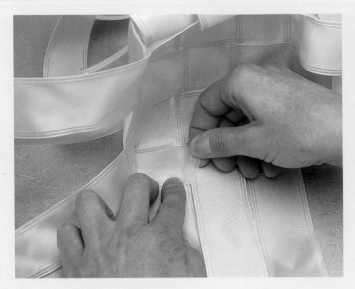

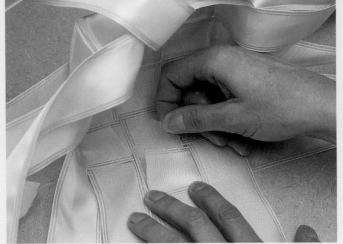

7 Complete First Row

When you have finished the fourth side of the first row, overlap the end of the ribbon onto the beginning square, place a square of fusible web underneath it and iron in place. Trim the end of the ribbon if needed. (Note: When weaving the ribbon around the body of the champagne pouch, lay it on a flat surface and make sure all ribbon strips are spaced evenly and tightly.)

8 Begin Second Row

Continuing the every-other-square technique, begin the second row by overlapping the end of the second-row ribbon over the center strip of base ribbon on the first side. Place a square of fusible web underneath it and iron it in place.

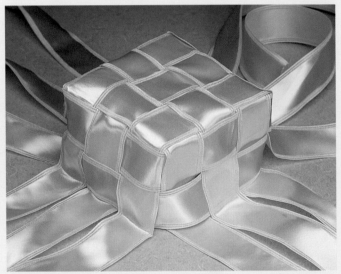

9 Weave Second Row

Continue weaving and fusing the strip of ribbon in the second row. The first side—the same side row one was started on—will be fused under the center square, the second side will be fused underneath the two outer squares, the third side will be fused under the center square, and the fourth side will be fused underneath the two outer squares. To complete the row, bring the ribbon around to the starting side and overlap the center square with the end of the ribbon. Fuse the end in place and trim if necessary.

10 Complete Second Row

The champagne pouch begins to take shape after the first two rows are complete. The pattern created by fusing underneath every other square causes an attractive dark and light shading on the satin ribbon squares.

11 Continue Weaving Rows

Continue weaving the body of the pouch. Rows three (shown here), five and seven are woven and fused the same as row one. Rows four, six and eight are woven and fused the same as row two.

12 Finish Weaving Top Row

Attach the end of the last row of ribbon by overlapping and inserting a square of fusible web and ironing it in place.

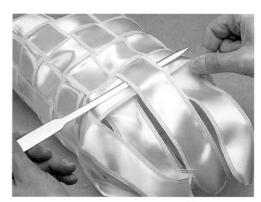

13 Fuse Top Row of Pouch

After the eighth row has been completed, the inner sections of the vertical ribbons need to be fused to the inside of the pouch. Use a letter opener or another tool to simulate the cording passing through the ribbon to avoid fusing a section of ribbon that needs to be left open. Place a sqare of fusible web between the ribbon sections and iron in place. On the first side, the fusible web will be underneath the center ribbon.

14 Complete Top Row

Continue fusing the inside top of the pouch. On the second side, the fusible web squares will be placed underneath the two outer squares as shown. Continue around to sides three and four, alternating squares.

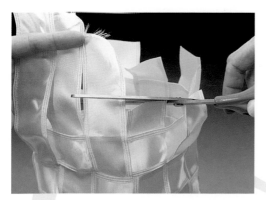

15 Trim Ribbon Ends

Measure and cut the ribbons coming out of the top of the champagne pouch to 1" (2.5cm). These will be folded over the inside of the pouch to form a smooth top edge.

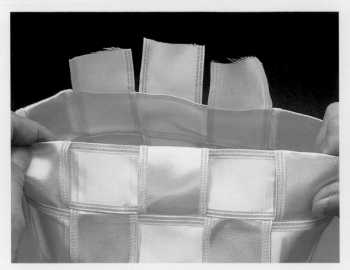

16 Form Top Edge

Bend each ribbon end toward the center of the pouch. Alternating squares will either bend over the last row of ribbon or back on themselves.

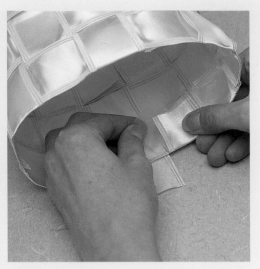

17 Fuse Ribbons

Place a piece of fusible web under each ribbon end and iron in place.

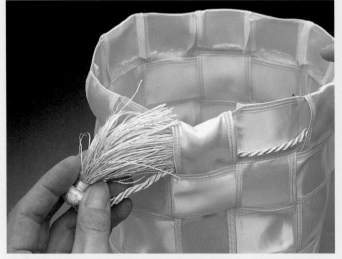

18 Insert Cording

Insert the cording into the top row of the champagne pouch by pushing the knot of the tassel through the open sections.

19 Thread Cording

Continue threading cording through the top sections.

20 *Complete Pouch Opening*

Continue threading the tassel through the sections until it is wrapped twice around the pouch top. Bring both ends out of the same opening and adjust until the tassels are even.

Completed Champagne Pouch

topiary
centerpiece

Create this stunning topiary full of fresh flowers that will later dry naturally to make a lovely keepsake of your wedding day. Designed with roses, heather, eucalyptus, berries and encircled with curly willow, this topiary makes a striking buffet table centerpiece.

difficulty 💍 💍 💍

cost *$50-100*

time ⏰ ⏰

→ **materials**

- 18 roses

- 6 stems heather

- 3 stems caspia

- 3 stems baby's breath

- 8–10 branches seeded eucalyptus

- 5–8 stems pepper berry

- 5–8 stems privet berry

- 3 branches curly willow

- sphagnum moss

- 1 small silk ivy bush

- foam topiary form

- green spray paint

- leaf shine spray

- floral adhesive

- floral picks

- decorative ribbon

- greening pins

- clay pot or other decorative plant container

1 *Paint Topiary Form*

Using green spray paint, paint the stem of the foam topiary form. This will help the stem blend into the arrangement.

2 *Glue Topiary Form to Pot*

Apply floral adhesive to the base of the foam topiary form where it will come into contact with the clay pot. Press the topiary into the clay pot and hold it until the glue is secure.

64

3 *Prepare the Base*

Soak the sphagnum moss in water until it is thoroughly wet. Gently wring out pieces of moss and place them on top of the base of the topiary to cover the foam form. If necessary, floral adhesive can be used to attach the moss securely.

4 *Drape Ivy Around Topiary*

Insert a stem of silk ivy into the top of the topiary. If the stem will not go into the foam form, poke a hole in the foam with a floral pick where the ivy stem is to be inserted. Secure the stem in the hole with floral adhesive. Drape the ivy down the side of the topiary top, wind around the stem to simulate a growing branch, and press the other end of the stem into the foam base through the moss. Use a floral pick to create a hole and floral adhesive if needed to secure the stem.

5 *Cover Topiary Ball With Ivy*

Add a second stem of ivy and secure one end at the top
of the topiary ball and the other end at the bottom of the
topiary ball. Continue adding ivy stems until the ball is
covered.

6 *Add Ivy to Topiary Base*

Insert additional stems of ivy into the topiary base and
drape them over the sides of the pot.

7 *Add Eucalyptus*

Cut sprigs of seeded eucalyptus and insert them into the
topiary ball until it is completely covered. Use the floral
pick to create holes for inserting stems and add floral
adhesive to hold the stems securely.

8 *Insert Eucalyptus in Topiary Base*

Add sprigs of seeded eucalyptus to
the topiary base and secure them
with greening pins.

9 *Add Privet Berries*

Cut sprigs of privet berries and insert them into the topiary as desired.

12 *Add Caspia*

Cut sprigs of caspia and use floral adhesive to insert them randomly in the topiary.

10 *Add Pepper Berries*

Cut sprigs of pepper berries and insert them into the topiary form as desired.

11 *Add Heather*

Cut sprigs of heather and insert them randomly throughout the topiary. If necessary, use a floral pick to create a hole and floral adhesive to secure the stems.

13 *Spray Leaf Shine*

Spray the entire topiary with leaf shine. This will help preserve the filler materials, keep them from drying out and bring out the colors.

14 *Add Roses*

Cut roses with 4" (10cm) stems and remove the thorns. Use a floral pick to make a hole and insert the roses randomly around the topiary ball. Use floral adhesive to secure the roses, especially those angled down. Add a rose or two to the base as well.

15 *Add Baby's Breath*

Cut stems of baby's breath and insert them randomly throughout the topiary ball and base. Use the floral pick and floral adhesive if necessary.

16 Add Curly Willow

Cut stems of curly willow long enough to easily wrap around the topiary ball and insert as desired. These stems may be cut short to stick out or longer to be wrapped around and inserted into the foam at both ends.

17 Attach Ribbon

Cut lengths of ribbon and fold one end over to form a loop. Use a greening pin to attach the loop to the base of the topiary ball, and arrange the streamers as desired.

18 Add Extra Streamers

Feel free to add extra streamers as I did in this topiary, to which three loops and streamers were added under the topiary ball. Most of the topiary can be made a week before the wedding, with the roses and baby's breath added 24 hours in advance of the reception. Store it in a cool place away from direct sun.

floral
napkin rings

Add a garden touch to your reception tables with these floral napkin rings. Inexpensive and easy to make, they can be matched to your wedding colors for a coordinated look.

❖ materials

- 1 silk mini carnation for each napkin ring

- 3 silk ranunculus blossoms for each napkin ring

- 2 silk yarrow clusters for each napkin ring

- 1 silk baby's breath stem for each napkin ring

- 1 silk statice stem for each napkin ring

- 1" to 1½" (2.5cm to 4 cm) wide plastic or wooden ring

- 1 yard (90cm) of ⅝" (16mm) wide white satin ribbon

- white floral tape

- floral adhesive

difficulty	💍
cost	< *$50*
time	⏰

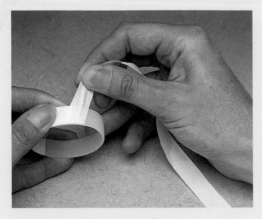

1 Wrap Ring

Wrap the entire ring with white floral tape, overlapping the tape slightly so it covers the whole surface.

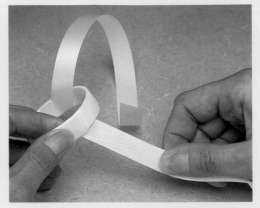

2 Add Ribbon

Wrap the entire ring with satin ribbon, leaving approximately 9" (23cm) ribbon streamers at the beginning and end.

3 Tie Ribbon Ends

After wrapping, tie the ribbon streamers snugly and make a shoestring bow. Trim the ribbon ends diagonally.

4 Cut Carnation Blossoms

Cut stems of miniature carnations and separate the individual blossoms from the stem base to make the flowers less bulky for gluing. Save the leaf stems for later.

5 Attach Carnation

Place a small dot of floral adhesive on the back of the carnation and wait a few moments until the glue gets tacky. Attach the carnation to the center of napkin ring bow.

6 Add Ranunculus

Glue three ranunculus blossoms around the carnation.

7 Add Yarrow

Glue two clusters of yarrow on either side of the flower cluster.

8 Add Statice

Glue individual buds of statice to fill in open spaces.

9 Add Baby's Breath

Fill in remaining open spaces with baby's breath.

10 Add Greenery

Embellish the floral cluster by adding leaves from the carnation stems.

Completed Napkin Ring

Write your
wedding wishes
to the
Bride & Groom.

message
basket & garland

Decorate your reception tables with lovely wicker baskets covered in flowers and ivy and filled with paper florets on which guests can write their wedding wishes to the happy couple. After the wedding, gather the florets and string them together to create a garland full of wedding memories that can be draped on a holiday tree, or on a mantle or stairway on anniversaries and special occasions.

difficulty

cost *$50-100*

time

▶ **materials**

- 3 stems silk button mums (various colors)
- 5–8 stems silk ivy
- potpourri
- handmade paper
- basket with handle
- double-sided ribbon, 1½" (4cm) wide minimum
- ½" (13mm) wide accent ribbon
- decoupage medium
- hot glue gun and glue
- stapler
- ½" (1cm) flat paint brush
- tissue paper
- wire cutters
- colored pencils or pens
- cording (for garland)

1 Form Bow

Leaving the ribbon on the spool, form a loop in the end of the ribbon. Add loops by holding the ribbon between the thumb and finger of one hand and forming the loops with the other hand.

2 Make Bow Loops

Continue forming loops on either side of the center loop, making each loop longer than the one before. Make a total of eight loops, four on each side.

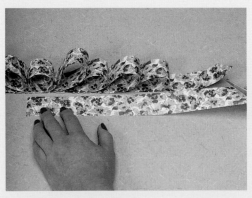

3 Adjust Bow to Basket

Hold the bow over the handle of the basket and adjust the loops to drape evenly over the handle. Make sure both sides are symmetrical. Next, trim the ribbon 4" or 5" (10cm or 13cm) beyond the longest loop using a diagonal or V-cut.

4 Staple Bow

Hold the ribbon firmly in one hand and staple the loops together in the center.

5 Cut Streamer

Lay the bow flat on a table and measure from the center of the bow to the end of the streamer and add 1" (2.5cm). Cut one streamer to that length.

6 Attach Streamer

Attach the streamer to the other side of the bow by stapling it into place as in step 4.

7 Attach Bow to Basket

Put a small amount of hot glue along the basket handle and let it set for 10 to 20 seconds. Press the bow into place and hold it until the glue is set.

8 Glue Bow Loops in Place

Starting with the bottom loops, use small dabs of hot glue to secure the loops in place. Secure each loop to the one below it.

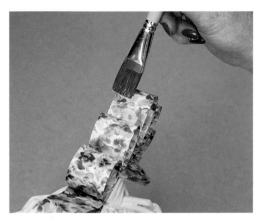

9 Decoupage Bow

Using a flat brush, coat the bow generously with decoupage medium. The decoupage medium will enrich the ribbon colors, create a glossy finish and add strength and durability to the ribbon. (Note: Test the decoupage medium on a section of ribbon before coating the bow. Some ribbons will darken when coated.)

10 Add Second Coat

Allow the decoupage medium to dry for the recommended time, then add a second coat. The type of ribbon used will determine how many coats will be needed before a nice, glossy finish is attained. To speed up the drying time, gently blow-dry.

11 *Add Ivy to Handle*

Cut sprigs of ivy and use hot glue to attach the stems around the bow along the basket handle.

12 *Add Ivy to Basket Base*

Glue ivy sprigs randomly around the rim of the basket. Push the stems through the basket weave and hold them in place until the hot glue takes hold.

Ivy Completed

13 Create Message Florets

Cut handmade paper into 6" x 6" (15cm x 15cm) squares. Fold the paper in half diagonally.

14 Fold in Half

Fold the paper in half again along the folded edge.

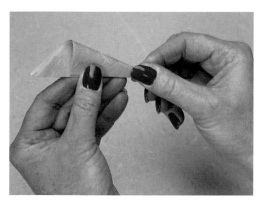

15 Fold Four Times

Locate the two folded edges. Fold again so that the two folded edges meet, creating a wedge shape. Repeat this fold two more times, keeping the folds as tight and precise as possible.

16 Round Edges

Cut a half circle into the wide end of the wedge making a shape like a slice of pie. Make sure to cut through all the layers of paper.

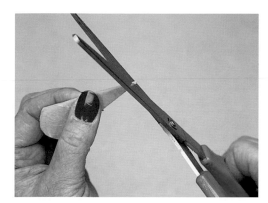

17 Cut Center Hole

Snip ⅛" (3mm) off the tip of the pie shape. Unfold the paper to reveal the floret.

18 Calculate the Number of Florets

If you plan to place one message basket on each reception table as a centerpiece, make 15 to 20 florets for every ten people. Two to four florets may be prewritten and strung from the message basket to serve as examples for the guests to follow, and a few extras should be included for people to write more than one if desired.

19 Fill the Basket

Crumple up a few pieces of white tissue paper and use them to fill the inside of the basket. Sprinkle potpourri on top of the tissue paper. Reserve some extra potpourri to sprinkle around the baskets once they are placed on the reception tables. Place the desired number of florets into the message basket.

78

20 Add Accent Ribbons

Cut two lengths of the accent ribbon so that the ends of each ribbon will flow onto the table from the top of the basket handle. The length of these ribbons will depend on the height of the basket. Thread the ribbons through the center loop on top of the message basket handle. Place a small amount of hot glue underneath the accent ribbons to anchor them to the handle.

21 Attach Sample Floret

Slide a sample floret onto an accent ribbon and tie a half-knot in the end of the ribbon to keep it in place.

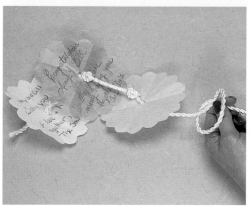

22 *Add Final Accents*

Cut one or two button mum stems and insert the flowers through the center hole of the floret and through the half-knot under the floret. Place the message baskets on the guest tables and arrange the floret samples around the baskets. Sprinkle potpourri on the table around the baskets. Add colored pencils or felt-tip pens for guests to write with. Placecards may be used to write instructions for the guests about the message baskets, or an announcement may be made during the reception.

23 *Make Garland*

After the wedding, gather up all the florets and make a keepsake garland. Attach the florets to the cording by tying a half-knot on either side of each floret. Space the florets 3" to 4" (8cm to 10cm) apart. The message garland can be brought out on anniversaries and holidays and used to drape over a doorway or mantle, adorn a stair railing or decorate a holiday tree.

Completed Message Basket and Garland

birdcage

card holder

Decorate a birdcage with lush silk roses, colorful

butterfly accents and elegant woven ribbon to create a

unique card holder inspired by the garden. Place it on

the gift table at the reception as a striking centerpiece.

▶ materials

- birdcage (wires should be spaced to allow large cards to pass through)

- 1 silk baby tears bush

- 1 silk rose bush with open roses (2 or more roses per stem)

- decorative butterflies

- double-sided woven ribbon

- foam floral cage

- green chenille stems

- floral adhesive

- wire cutters

difficulty   💍 💍

cost   *$50-100*

time   ⏰ ⏰

1 *Remove Swing*

Determine how the swing is attached and remove it. If necessary, use wire cutters to snip the swing attachment.

2 *Add Baby Tears*

Cut three stems of various lengths from the baby tears bush. (Stems must be long enough to drape over top half of birdcage.) Wrap the stem ends around the top of the birdcage and twist them securely around the top finial.

82

3 *Intertwine Stems*

Intertwine the stems around the wires of the birdcage, draping them around the top half of the cage. Avoid twining stems over the door, since the door will need to be opened to remove envelopes after the reception.

4 *Secure Stems*

Bring the ends of the baby tear stems down around the sides of the birdcage and continue winding the stems around the birdcage. If necessary, use green chenille stems to secure the stems to the birdcage, trimming or tucking the ends out of sight. (Note: Make sure there are enough clear spaces in the wire cage for people to pass standard size envelopes through to the inside.)

5 *Add Baby Tears to Birdcage Base*

Placing baby tear stems around the base of the birdcage is optional. If desired, wrap the stems around the base of the birdcage and intertwine the stems up the sides.

6 *Complete Greenery*

Continue adding baby tear stems until the desired effect is reached. To fill holes, trim small stems and add them by intertwining them with the longer stems or wrapping them into place with a chenille stem. Leave the door and surrounding area free and clear of greenery.

7 *Insert Large Rose*

Cut one large open rose from the bush, leaving approximately 2½" (6cm) of stem. Insert the rose into the front side of the floral foam cage.

8 *Add Smaller Roses*

Cut two smaller roses from the bush and leave approximately 1" (2.5cm) of stem. Insert one rose on each side of the larger rose, placing one higher than the other. Don't forget to keep the floral foam arrangement compact enough to fit through the birdcage door.

9 *Insert Center Rosebud*

Cut a small rosebud from the bush, leaving approximately 3" (8cm) of stem. Insert the rosebud in the center of the other three roses, pointing up.

10 *Add Leaves*

Cut sprigs of rose leaves and insert them into the floral foam cage as greenery around the roses. Fill in with the leaves until the cage is covered.

11 *Add Adhesive to Floral Cage*

Squeeze a generous amount of floral adhesive onto the bottom of the floral cage arrangement. Let the glue set for a few minutes until it gets tacky.

12 *Add Adhesive to Birdcage*

Squeeze a puddle of floral adhesive onto the center of the floor of the birdcage and let the glue set for a few minutes until it gets tacky.

13 *Place Arrangement in Birdcage*

Gently push the arrangement through the birdcage door, center it in the middle of the birdcage and glue it into place. Carefully cut the wire from the butterfly and glue it to one of the rose petals.
(Note: The birdcage door may be closed at this time. Wrap a branch of garland around the closure to secure the door until after the wedding.)

14 *Add Rose Stem to Birdcage Top*

Place a double stem of open roses through the hanger and around the top of the birdcage so the stems hang down on either side. Twist the stems to arrange the flowers as desired. Do not wire or glue them in place at this time.

15 *Add Second Rose Stem*

Insert a second double stem of roses through the opposite side of the birdcage hanger. Drape the stems down over the top of the birdcage perpendicular to the first stem. Press down on all the rose stems and mold them to the shape of the birdcage. (Note: If you want to use other flowers besides roses, any multibranch flower will work. Or wire single flower stems to the birdcage with chenille stems.)

16 Add Single Rose

Wrap a leftover single stem rose around the top of the birdcage on top of the other stems. Wrap it securely in place and arrange as desired.

17 Secure Flowers

When the flowers are arranged as desired, cut small lengths of chenille stem and twist them around the flower stems where they touch the birdcage. Trim any excess wire. Bend the wires back under the foliage to hide the ends. Glue a butterfly to one of the roses.

18 Add Bow

Use 4 yards (3.6m) of ribbon to make a bow (see bow instructions on page 27). Make the bow loops in varying sizes to drape over the top of the birdcage. Cut an additional 36" (90cm) length of ribbon and make two extra streamers. Wire the streamers into the bow with a green chenille stem. Anchor the bow to the birdcage by wrapping chenille stems securely around the top of the cage. Bend the ends into the foliage to conceal them.

19 Arrange Bow

Pull half of the bow loops through the birdcage hanger. Arrange the loops and streamers as desired and trim the ends of the streamers.

table wreath

Transform your reception tables with table wreaths illuminated by candlelight. Decorated with silk delphinium, silk button mums, silk yarrow, silk ivy and accented with ribbon, table wreaths can brighten up your guest tables, then be given away as keepsake gifts after the reception.

❧ materials

- 2 stems silk delphinium

- 6 stems silk yarrow (two colors)

- 4 stems silk button mums (two colors)

- silk ivy bush (medium size)

- sheet moss

- pillar candle

- 14" (36cm) foam wreath

- 1¹/₂" (4cm) wide sheer white ribbon

- ⁵/₈" (16mm) wide wired gold ribbon

- 24-gauge floral wire

- floral adhesive

- wire cutters

difficulty	
cost	< $50
time	

1 *Apply Adhesive*

Cover the entire top of the wreath with floral adhesive. (Allow the adhesive to drip down the sides.) Let the adhesive set for approximately five minutes until it's tacky.

2 *Soak Moss*

Soak sheet moss in water. After the moss is completely soaked through, gently squeeze the excess water out with your hands.

3 *Apply Moss*

Apply the moss to the floral ring until the ring is completely covered on the top and sides.

4 *Add Ivy*

Cut small sprigs of ivy and insert them into the wreath, leaving small areas where moss shows through.

5 Add Yarrow

Cut three sprigs of each color of yarrow and insert the stems, alternating colors.

6 Add Delphinium

Cut delphinium stems into four small sections and insert them into the ring.

7 Add Button Mums

Cut individual stems of button mums and dip the stems in floral adhesive. Randomly insert them into the floral ring.

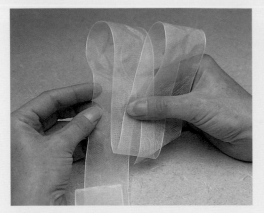

8 Make Sheer Bows

To add small ribbon bows, cut four strips of sheer ribbon approximately 30" (76cm) long. Form the bow by making two loops in one end of the ribbon.

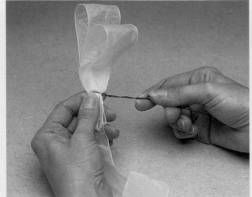

9 Wire Bows

Pinch the ribbon loops together at the base and wrap them with wire to secure. Twist the ends of the wire and trim the excess, leaving approximately 4" (10cm) of wire stem.

10 Insert Bows

Insert the four bows into the wreath by pushing the twisted wire stems into the foam where desired.

11 Insert Gold Bows

Make four additional bows out of the gold ribbon using the technique in steps 8 and 9. Insert the gold bows into the wreath as desired.

12 *Make Ribbon Tails*

Cut four 8" (20cm) lengths of gold ribbon. To make a ribbon tail, wrap a wire around the center and twist to secure.

13 *Tie Ribbon*

Tie a knot in the ribbon and pull the ends gently. Trim the ends of the wire to approximately 4" (10cm).

14 *Insert Ribbon Tails*

Insert the four ribbon tails around the wreath as desired.

Completed Table Wreath With Candle

bride & groom
chairs

Drape ordinary chairs in yards of elegant fabric to create dramatic bride and groom chairs for the head table. Finish them off with fancy satin ribbons and lush silk roses for a touch of romance.

difficulty 💍 💍 💍 💍 💍

cost > *$100*

time 🕐 🕐 🕐

❖ **materials**

- 4–6 silk rose sprays (2 or more flowers per stem)

- 1 small silk ivy bush

- 48"–60" (1.2m–1.5m) of fabric per chair (heavy, non-wrinkle upholstery grade brocade, cotton chintz or moiré; no sheer or satin)

- no. 40 ivory satin ribbon (2 yards [1.8m] for each chair)

- coordinating wide, fancy satin ribbon for bow (5–6 yards [4.5m–5.4m] for each chair)

- 2" (5cm) and 1½" (4cm) corsage pins

- cable ties

- chenille stems

- 1" (2.5cm) wide fusible seam tape

- safety pins

- wire cutters

1 Measure Fabric

To make sure the fabric is the proper size for the chair being covered, drape the fabric evenly over the chair. Make sure the raw edges of the fabric touch the floor all the way around the chair and there is at least 6" (15cm) of excess fabric on all sides. Trim the fabric if necessary. Pin up a 1" (2.5cm) hem on all sides of the fabric and iron flat.

2 Create Seam

Remove the pins and fold the fabric edge over again to form a 1" (2.5cm) seam with a finished edge. Pin and iron flat.

3 Place Seam Tape

Remove the pins and cut lengths of fusible seam tape to lay along the edges of the fabric seam.

94

4 Fuse Seam

Fold the fabric over once more so the fusible seam tape is underneath the folded edge. Pin the seam if necessary and iron it until the fusible seam tape is activated and secures the finished fabric edge.

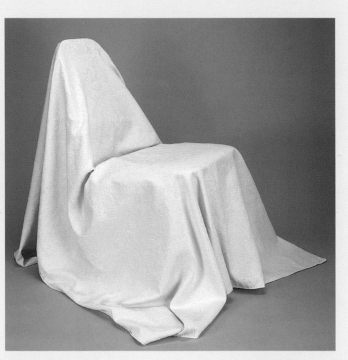

5 Drape Chair

Drape the hemmed fabric over the chair and arrange it so that all of the edges are touching the floor.

6 Create Side Panels

Pull the fabric by one front chair leg flush with the chair back so that the fabric hangs evenly across the front and side of the chair. Pin the fabric to hold it in place. Repeat this for the opposite side.

7 Cover Side Seam

Pull the excess fabric that is draped over the back of the chair forward to cover the side seam and pin in place. Repeat this for the opposite side.

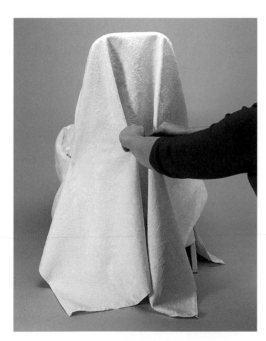

8 Overlap Back Folds

Pull the two center back folds together and overlap them. Secure them underneath with safety pins.

9 Wrap Ribbon Around Chair

Wrap the no. 40 satin ribbon around the chair back and tie it with a square knot. Leave enough ribbon to form streamers and let them drape almost to the floor.

Completed Groom Chair

10 *Add Bow*

Using the techniques on page 27, make a large bow out of the satin ribbon. For the groom's chair, pin the bow to the back of the chair over the square knot. Now the groom's chair is finished! Do not secure a bow to the bride's chair yet—proceed to step 11.

11 *Begin Bouquet*

To make the floral bouquet, start with the small ivy bush and add three stems of roses. Arrange the roses in a triangle pattern and weave the ivy stems between the flowers.

12 *Gather Flowers*

Add three shorter stemmed roses and wrap all the stems securely with a cable tie. Cut off the excess tie end. Trim the stems if necessary to approximately 8" to 10" (20cm to 25cm).

13 *Wrap Stems*

Starting at the base of the bouquet, wrap the stems tightly with the no. 40 satin ribbon.

14 *Secure Ribbon*

At the top of the stems, trim the ribbon, fold over the end and pin it securely with two or three corsage pins.

15 *Attach Bow to Bouquet*

Attach the bow from step 10 to the front of the bouquet with a chenille stem.

16 *Attach Bouquet to Chair*

Slide the bouquet stems inside the chair ribbon. Pin individual flowers and ivy stems to the chair fabric where necessary to secure the bouquet in place.

Completed Bride Chair

origami
cranes

Because they mate for life, cranes are an important symbol in Japanese wedding tradition. Fold 1,001 origami cranes and you'll enjoy a long married life together and good luck a thousand times over. Use these elegant cranes to decorate reception tables or hang them from a wedding arch.

▸materials

• origami paper in assorted colors

difficulty 💍 💍 💍

cost   < $50

time   🕐

1 *Fold Diagonally*

Fold a perfectly square sheet of origami paper diagonally in half, lining it up corner to corner to form a triangle.

2 *Fold Into a Triangle*

Fold the paper again into an even smaller triangle.

3 *Open Flap*

Lay the paper open to the first triangle and open the flap. Flatten the flap to a square and turn it over.

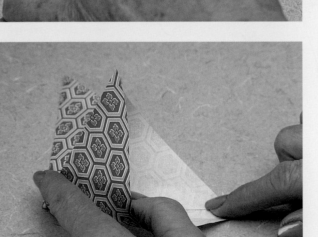

4 Open Second Flap

Open up the other flap and flatten it to a square. You should now have a perfect square.

5 Fold First Corner

Fold one corner of the square so that the edge is lined up with the center line.

6 Fold Second Corner

Repeat step 5 with the other flap to form a triangle in the center.

7 *Complete Four Corners*

Flip the paper over and repeat steps 5 and 6 for the other two flaps.

8 *Lift Top Flap*

Lift the top flap on the open end and fold it upward.

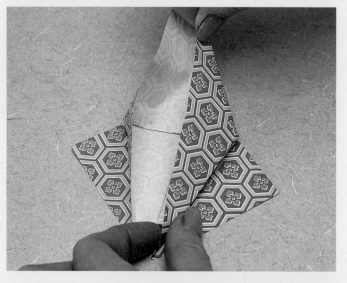

9 *Lay Flat*

Lay the flap flat, creating a diamond shape.

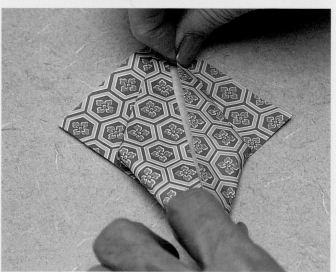

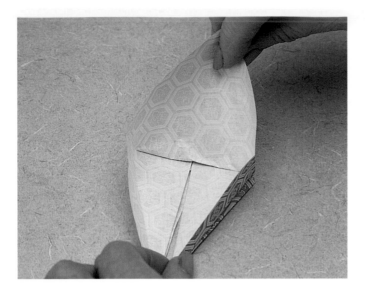

10 *Create Diamond Shape*

Flip the paper over and repeat steps 8 and 9 on the other side.

11 *Fold Toward Center*

With the open end pointing toward you, fold in one flap so that the edge lines up with the center line.

12 *Complete All Center Flaps*

Repeat step 11 for the other flap so both flaps are lined up along the center. Flip the paper over and repeat this for both flaps on the other side.

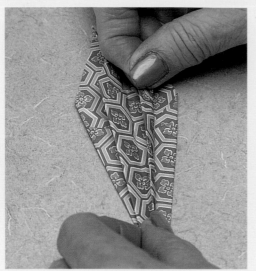

13 *Turn Right Flap*
Turn the right flap to the left and lay it flat.

14 *Turn Left Flap*
Repeat step 13 on the other side and lay it flat.

15 *Make Wings*
Pull the bottom flat flap up all the way to form the first wing. Repeat this on the other side.

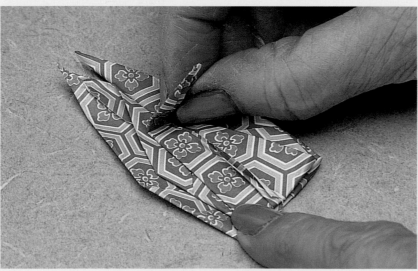

16 *Form Head and Tail*
Invert one of the upper tips to form the head. Pull back the opposite tip to form the tail.

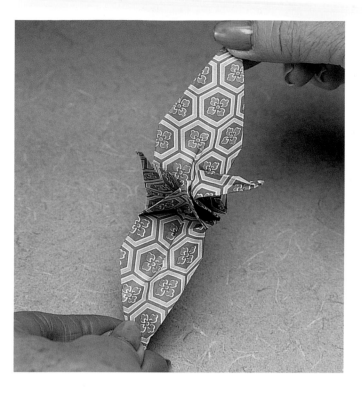

17 *Form Body*

Gently pull the wings apart to form the body.

Completed Origami Cranes

three

Treasured keepsakes that preserve memories of your wedding day will always hold a special place in your heart. This chapter will show you creative ways to save pictures and mementos that you will cherish forever. Design a beautifully bound memory book to save programs, cards, photographs and wedding wishes that celebrate your special day. Elegantly display your wedding invitation preserved in a dried floral wreath. Create picture frames delicately embellished with flowers and ribbon to be given as gifts to family members with candid photographs of your wedding. Preserve your wedding bouquet through various drying methods that allow you to keep it long after your wedding. There are so many creative and imaginative ways to capture the romance of this happy occasion. Create something to help your memories last a lifetime.

cherished
memories

memory book

Embellish a store-bought wedding memory book, guestbook or photo album with elegant fabric, ribbons and silk blossoms to create a personalized keepsake. This beautiful book is the perfect place to save engagement and wedding mementos, cherished photographs and guest wishes.

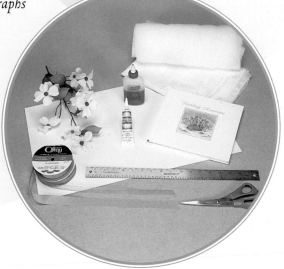

difficulty 💍 💍 💍

cost *$50-100*

time 🕐 🕐 🕐

> **materials**

- spiral-bound memory book, photo album, scrapbook or guest book (we used a 9 ½" x 8 ½" [24cm x 22cm] memory book)

- 1–2 yards (91cm–183cm) of decorative moiré fabric depending on book size (we used 1 yard [91cm] of 54" [137cm] wide moiré for our book size)

- 1 stem silk dogwood (or silk flower of choice)

- ⁷⁄₈" (22mm) wide grosgrain ribbon (we used 2 yards [183cm] for our book size)

- ⁵⁄₈" (16mm) wide sheer ribbon

- 1 yard (91cm) of quilt batting

- posterboard

- fabric glue

- floral adhesive

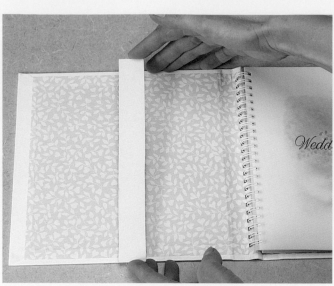

1 Measure Cover Fabric

Measure the height and width of the book cover. (The fabric should come within ¼" (6mm) of the spirals.) Add 1" (2.5cm) to all sides and cut two pieces of fabric to size, one for the front cover and one for the back. (Note: If using a fabric with a pattern or grain, make sure the fabric matches on both front and back pieces.)

2 Reinforce Edge

Cut two 1" (2.5cm) wide strips of posterboard the same height as the book cover.

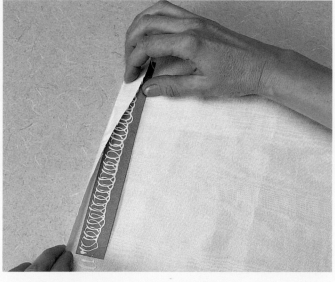

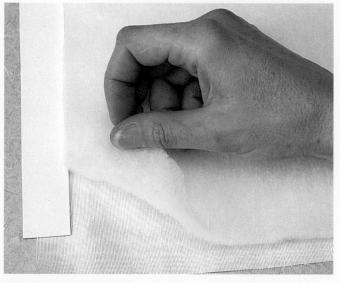

3 Glue Edge

Turn the fabric face down, making sure your pattern or grain runs from top to bottom. Place the posterboard strip ½" (13mm) from the edge of the fabric. (Make sure the strip is evenly spaced between the top and bottom of the fabric.) Apply fabric glue to the back of the posterboard strip, fold the ½" (13mm) edge of fabric onto the strip and glue into place.

4 Insert Quilt Batting

Unfold the glued posterboard strip so the fabric once again lies flat with the wrong side face up. Cut a piece of quilt batting that is ½" (13mm) shorter on three sides than the fabric with the batting up against the inside edge of the posterboard strip.

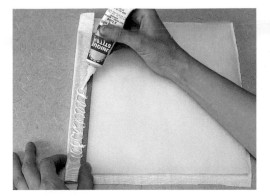

5 Form the Cover's Edge

Fold the posterboard strip over onto the fabric, sandwiching the batting between the strip and the fabric. Apply fabric glue along the strip.

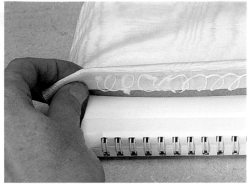

6 Attach Cover

Carefully glue the edged fabric to the cover of the guest-book. The edge with the posterboard strip should lie next to the spiral binding on both front and back. Place a heavy weight on it until the glue is set securely.

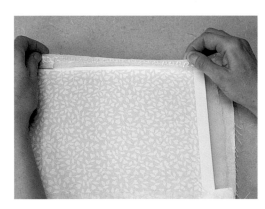

7 Finish Top and Bottom Edges

Open the guest book and lay the cover flat. Apply fabric glue to the top and bottom edges of the fabric and fold them over onto the inside cover of the book. Smooth the fabric with your fingers until the glue has securely anchored the fabric to the cover.

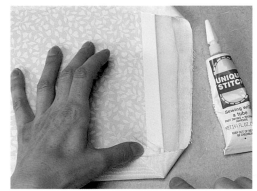

8 Fold Corners

Fold the corners as shown to create finished edges. Apply fabric glue under the folds to secure the fabric.

9 Finish Outer Edge

Apply fabric glue to the outside edge of the fabric and fold it over onto the cover, making sure the corners are tightly folded. Smooth the fabric with your fingers until the glue has securely anchored the fabric to the cover.

10 Cut Inside Cover Board

Cut a piece of posterboard slightly smaller than the inside cover.

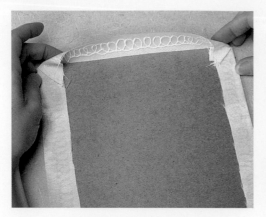

11 Glue Fabric to Board

Cut a piece of fabric large enough that each side overlaps the posterboard by 1" (2.5cm). Make sure to properly orient any fabric pattern or grain. Apply fabric glue to the edges of the fabric and fold them over onto the back side of the posterboard using the corner technique in steps 7–9. Do not glue the fabric to the front of the posterboard.

12 Glue Board to Inside Cover

Apply fabric glue to the back side of the posterboard and glue it into place on the inside book cover. Place a heavy weight on it until the glue has completely adhered.

13 Complete Inside Covers

Repeat steps 11 and 12 for the back cover. Make sure to properly orient any fabric pattern or grain.

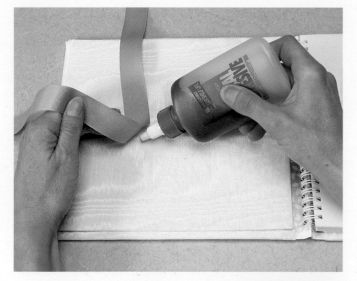

14 Wrap Ribbon Around Cover

Wrap a piece of grosgrain ribbon lengthwise completely around the front cover (length will vary according to book size) and cut it so the ends overlap by 1" (2.5cm). Offset the ribbon slightly to the outside of the guest book. On the inside of the front cover, place a small amount of floral adhesive on the center of the ribbon to secure.

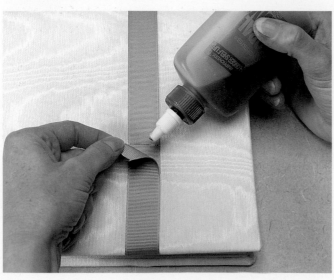

15 Attach Ribbon Ends

Bring the ribbon ends around to the front of the book cover and glue them in place with a little bit of floral adhesive. Make sure the ends overlap at the point where the bow will be placed.

16 *Add Bow*

Cut a 28" (71cm) length of grosgrain ribbon and glue the center to the cover ribbon with floral adhesive. When the adhesive has set securely, tie a shoestring bow, making the loops 1" (2.5cm) longer than the desired final length.

17 *Add Flowers*

Cut two dogwood blossoms with 2" (5mm) of stem. Try to find flowers with leaves close to them if possible. Lay the stems opposite each other over the center of the bow.

18 *Secure Flowers*

Double-knot the shoestring bow around the flower stems.

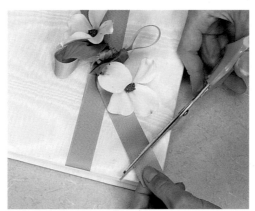

19 *Finish Off Bow*

Adjust the flowers and bow loops as desired. Trim the ribbon ends with diagonal cuts.

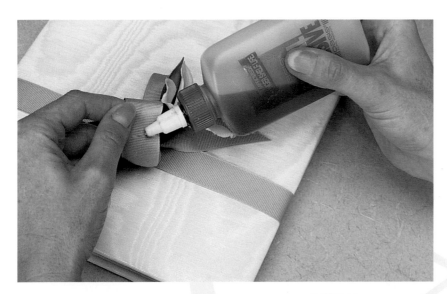

20 *Arrange Bow*

Place a small amount of floral adhesive on the ends of the ribbons and ribbon loops and let the glue set for a few minutes until it gets tacky. Gently press the ribbon ends and loops into place on the cover.

(Note: Place only a small amount of glue on the ribbons. Test a sample piece to make sure the glue will not bleed through the ribbon.)

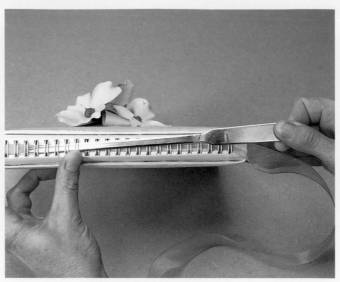

21 Add Flowers

If desired, add more dogwood blossoms around the bow. Glue one or two petals of each blossom to the cover to hold it in place.

22 Thread Ribbon for Bookmark

Leaving the sheer ribbon on the roll, thread the ribbon inside the spiral binding. (It is helpful to open the guestbook to relieve pressure on the spirals.) A letter opener or tweezers may be useful to help thread the ribbon. The ribbon extending out of the bottom of the spirals should be trimmed to approximately 6" (15cm). Trim the other end to approximately twice the height of the book.

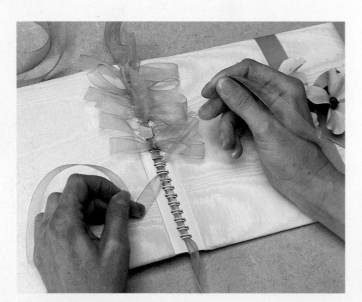

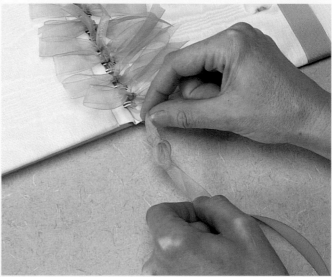

23 Add Bows to Spine

Cut several 18" (46cm) lengths of sheer ribbon. The number of bows needed will depend on the size of your book and the number of spirals you decide to wrap with a bow. In this example, we wrapped every two spirals with a bow. Count the spirals ahead of time and plan how many spirals you will wrap. Thread the ribbon under the spirals and center it. Tie shoestring bows, lining up the loops to a little longer than the desired finished size. Double knot the loops and trim the ribbon ends with diagonal cuts as you move down the spine.

24 Knot Ribbon

Loosely tie a slip knot in the ribbon that extends through the bottom of the spirals to prevent the ribbon from sliding out. If the spirals are large, make a square knot or bow to anchor the ribbon.

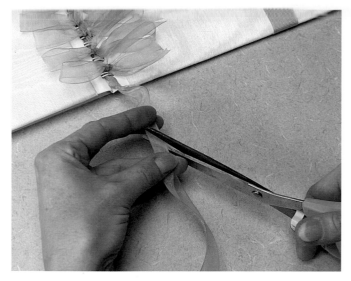

25 *Finish Off Ribbon End*

Pull the ribbon up through the spirals until the knot is at the base of the spirals. Trim the end of the ribbon with a V-cut by folding the ribbon in half and cutting diagonally.

26 *Complete Bookmark*

Open the guest book and bring the other end of the bookmark ribbon down over the center of the book. Attach a single dogwood blossom with floral adhesive below where the bookmark extends beyond the pages. Trim the end of the ribbon with a V-cut 3" (8cm) below the blossom.

Completed Keepsake Book

wedding
keepsake wreath

Create a keepsake wreath commemorating your wedding day that you will cherish for many years to come. In addition to featuring your wedding invitation and dried flowers, include preserved flowers from your bridal bouquet and reception centerpieces for a personal touch.

difficulty 💍 💍

cost *$50-100*

time 🕐 🕐

▶ **materials**

- dried baby's breath

- seeded eucalyptus (dried or fresh)

- dried German statice

- dried caspia

- dried delphinium

- eucalyptus

- dried statice

- wedding invitation

- 1½" (4cm) wide wired ribbon

- ⅝" (16mm) wide sheer ribbon

- floral foam ring (9" [23cm] ring pictured)

- clear acrylic gloss spray

- paper punch

- floral adhesive

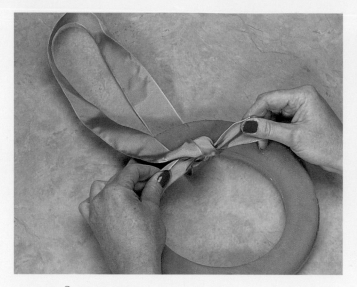

1 Make Wreath Hanger

Cut a piece of wired ribbon 36" (90cm) long. Pull the ribbon through the floral foam ring and tie a square knot. Trim ends as desired. The size of the floral ring needed for this project will depend upon the size of your wedding invitation. I used a 9" (23cm) wreath.

2 Insert Seeded Eucalyptus

Cut small sprigs of seeded eucalyptus and fill in the floral ring. Push the stems into the floral ring at least 1" (2.5cm). (Note: Push the stems into the floral foam at an angle for added security, so that when the wreath is hanging, the stems won't fall out.) If any of the stems do not anchor firmly into the floral foam, place a little floral adhesive on the stems before reinserting.

3 Spray With Clear Gloss

When the foam ring has been completely covered with seeded eucalyptus, spray the wreath with clear acrylic gloss. This should be done outside or in a well-ventilated area to avoid accumulation of fumes. Fold the ribbon hanger up behind the wreath when spraying to avoid spraying the ribbon.

4 Place Invitation

Place the invitation on top of the wreath and make sure proportions and shape are as desired.

5 Punch Holes

Working from the back side of the invitation, measure the card for placement of two holes each at the top and bottom, 1" (2.5cm) apart. Find the center point of the invitation and make a small mark 1/2" (13mm) on either side of the center point. Punch out the holes with a paper punch.

6 Spray Invitation

Spray both sides of the invitation with clear acylic gloss to preserve it.

7 Add Bows

Cut two 24" (61cm) lengths of 5/8" (16mm) sheer ribbon. Thread the ribbon through the holes and tie a bow at the top and bottom. Double-knot the loops.

8 Apply Adhesive

Apply floral adhesive to the back of the invitation and let the glue set for a few minutes until it is tacky.

9 Attach Invitation to Wreath

Press the invitation firmly into the wreath until it is secured.

10 *Add Eucalyptus*

Cut small sprigs of eucalyptus and clean the the leaves from the bottom portion of the stems. Insert the stems at an angle randomly throughout the wreath.

11 *Add Caspia*

Cut small sprigs of caspia and insert the stems at an angle into the wreath as desired. Use floral adhesive on the stems if necessary.

12 *Add Baby's Breath*

Cut small sprigs of baby's breath and insert the stems into the wreath as desired. Use floral adhesive on the stems if necessary.

13 *Add Statice*

Cut small sprigs of various colors of statice and insert them at an angle into the wreath as desired.

14 *Add German Statice*

Cut small sprigs of German statice and insert them at an angle into the wreath as desired.

15 *Add Delphinium*

Cut small sprigs of various colors of delphinium and insert them at an angle into wreath as desired. Because dried delphinium is extremely fragile, use floral adhesive to place it in the wreath.

16 *Spray the Wreath*

Lay the wreath flat on a covered surface or outside and spray the entire arrangement with clear acrylic gloss spray to help preserve the flowers. (Avoid spraying the ribbon hangar.)

Completed Keepsake Wreath

picture frame

Customize inexpensive picture frames with decorative
ribbon and dried flowers to showcase informal photographs from the wedding. Simple to create, this picture
frame makes a lovely keepsake for the wedding couple
or a cherished gift for family and friends.

▶ materials

- dried delphinium

- dried hydrangea

- preserved plumosa

- 5" x 7" (13cm x 18cm) clear acrylic picture frame

- 2' (61cm) of ¼" (6mm) wide gold ribbon

- floral adhesive

difficulty	💍 💍
cost	< *$50*
time	🕐

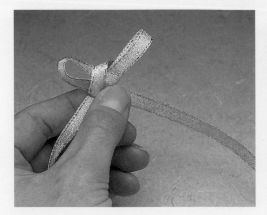

1 Tie Ribbon

Tie a shoestring bow in the middle of the ribbon, keeping the loops small. Pull the loops tight to knot the center.

2 Attach Bow

Place a dot of floral adhesive on the back of the knot and stick the ribbon to the frame at an angle in the upper left-hand corner.

3 Add Ribbon Spirals

Twist the ribbon ends to create spirals. One end of the ribbon will spiral across the top of the frame, while the other will spiral down the left side of the frame. Apply floral adhesive to the back of the first twist of ribbon where it will make contact with the frame and press it into place. Use a pipe cleaner or another thin stick to help apply glue and attach the ribbon spirals. Continue twisting and attaching loops until the edge of the frame is reached, then trim the ribbon with a diagonal cut.

4 Add Greenery

Trim and glue tips of plumosa stems around the center of the bow.

5 Add Delphinium

Cut individual delphinium blossoms from the stalk. Handle the dried flowers carefully to avoid crumbling them. Place a small amount of glue on the back of each blossom and attach them where the ribbon loops touch the frame. Cut a few unopened buds along with stems to use around the center of the bow.

6 Add Hydrangea

Cut individual hydrangea blossoms, place a small amount of glue on the back of each one and place them along the ribbon as desired.

Completed Keepsake Photo Frame

preserving your wedding flowers

fresh bridal bouquet

Drying Flowers

There are many ways to preserve the flowers from your bouquet, ceremony or reception arrangements. Flowers can be air-dried, dried in silica gel or preserved through an advanced process called freeze-drying. Air-dried and freeze-dried flowers may be dried with the stems attached, while flowers are dried in silica gel without the stems.

Air-Drying

While there are several methods of air-drying flowers, hanging them upside down in a dark, dry and well-ventilated place will dry most varieties. When dry, the flowers will be smaller than their original size, color may be lost and the petals and leaves will have a wrinkled appearance. Most flowers dry within five days to two weeks.

Silica Gel

Available in most craft stores, silica gel is a powder that dries flower heads to a nearly fresh appearance within several days. It absorbs moisture from the flowers while supporting their natural shape. Silica gel can also be reused several times. Simply place the flower heads face up in a container partially filled with the silica gel powder, preferably an airtight container that is shallow and large in diameter. Gently sprinkle silica gel between the flower petals, then cover the flowers complete-

ly with the powder. Tightly cover the container with a lid and allow the flowers to dry for two to seven days. The process must be checked daily so the flowers do not overdry and become brittle. Finally, remove the dried flowers with a slotted spoon, gently lifting them from the powder. Remove the excess silica gel from the flower petals with a soft brush. These flowers can now be used for arranging, but will need to have wire stems added for support.

Freeze-Drying

Freeze-drying is a relatively new and advanced drying process that can preserve a flower almost indefinitely. Freeze-dried flowers keep their shape and color, can be used easily in arrangements, and the stem never has to be cut from the flower head. To have your flowers freeze-dried, take them to a professional florist who specializes in this process. Check the resource page to locate a florist near you with this expertise.

Freeze-drying has become known as a near-perfect method of flower preservation. The freeze-drier removes the water from the flower at subzero temperatures through a vacuum. The moisture is collected in a condensation chamber and defrosted throughout the preservation time. The flowers are then warmed to room temperature. The whole process takes 10 to 15 days. This slow process allows the flowers to hold their natural size and shape, as well as their vibrant color. Love may be eternal, but most wedding bouquets die quickly. The freeze-drying process can keep your wedding bouquet looking as beautiful as the day you carried it down the aisle.

freeze-dried bouquet